Poems From the Thin Places

Monica R. Lavia

This book is dedicated to
Matteo, Mario, Emilia, Quinn and Grace
The ones who bring joy to my life

Table of Contents

Response to Suscipe

WITH MY APOLOGIES TO IGNATIUS

Please Lord,
Give me back all my liberty,
My memory, my understanding,
My entire will.
Do not forget how strong willed I am.
Remember to give me back please
My whole entire will.
All that I have and call my own,
I still have and call my own.
You have given all to me, and I accept it.
To you, Lord, I might or might not, return it some day.
Do you see, you cannot do with it as you will.
I would like to say you can, but I am afraid.
Give me a job, health, family, friends and security.
Give me your love and your grace also.
I am American, I want it all.

Planting Tomatoes

Little seedlings bedded in a flat
Are held firmly in my hand
As I round the side of the house
And at the site already chosen
I lower myself onto this ground
Sitting on the warm hill of earth
Late morning sun at my back
I begin to turn dirt
At first with my hand trowel
Then just with my hands
Digging and Scooping
Sifting clumps through my fingers
Feeling the fine softness of the rich dark soil
I close my eyes and am transported

I think of those who made their lives here
Thousands of years before I
came to be in this place
Generations of families who sheltered, protected
And sometimes buried their young here
I am filled with a sense of the joy and the grief
In the lives of these peoples, and suddenly,
With warm earth sifting through my fingers
I grasp the connection
The bodies of those who have gone before me have
Nourished this soil and thus are we are bonded
Because the fruits of this same soil
Will nourish the bodies of those
Who with joy and grief and work
Have come to be in this place
In the now of this present moment

Thoughts While Holding Quinn

A GRANDSON BORN TOO SOON

child of my child
I gaze upon you
a vision of perfection
in exquisitely created miniature.
I hold your flawless sculpted
not ready to be birthed body.
translucent baby skin presses next to mine
melting into me.
swaddled in my arms Quinn
does any memory surface?
I long to know do you recall
that sensation of
being swaddled
in the hand of God?

babe of my babe
I feel your tiny puffs
in and out rise and fall
inhaled goodness exhaled knowledge.
I kiss your head your cheek your hand
pressing you to me I inhale your scent
the sweet infant perfume
of innocence and purity.
as you relax into my arms Quinn
does memory stir?
do you still possess
any recollection of
that healing quiet comfort of
resting in the breath of God?

tiny teacher of mine
I have so much to learn from you
tolerance of pain acceptance of injustice
my pain is that of a mother watching
her child suffer who watches her child suffer
Quinn it just hurts so much
come with me now
I hold you securely
together we will go
to the secret place of healing comfort.
the place where He blends our woundedness with His
He lifts and places us into the wound in His side
nothing can harm or hurt us now
we will be at peace and rest.

The Spirit of Kate

Entering the house I stand in the foyer and remove my shoes in response
To an inner sensation that I stand on holy ground.
Holy ground of plain hard wood floor, in this simple Raleigh ranch.
Glancing to my right, in the darkening shadows of dusk I can see a
Fertile mother and her trio of new life.
The music of innocent unpracticed infant laughter reaches me in triplicate
And I once again recall the words of Meister Eckhart:

When the Father laughs at the Son and the Son laughs back at the Father,
that laughter gives pleasure and that pleasure gives joy.
That joy gives love, and that love is the Holy Spirit.

I fix my sight on her as she beholds her three little ones
Is it true that the begotten is one with the creator?
Then is this co-creator one with this trinity of her flesh?
Standing back in the shadows I reverently watch
The threesome fix their gaze on her
Their eyes lock on the features of her face
She smiles to each of them and to all of them
The triad smile and laugh in response.
I witness laughter, pleasure, joy and love
A tangible love that is almost palpable
An interior hush falls over my senses and my soul quiets in awe.
I do believe that I have just seen
The holy spirit of Kate.

Christmas Shopping

I dreamed I went Christmas shopping with Jesus last week
We were at Triangle Town Center, I sat next to Him on a bench.
Not in the expected white robe and sandals garb
He wore brown wool flannel pants, Brooks Brothers I think
And a camel colored cashmere sweater, so soft to the touch.
He had aged a bit, perhaps from His crucifixion.
I have heard that crucifixion will do that to you.

Jesus asked me what I wanted for Christmas.
I was surprised to hear myself saying I wanted peace.
The kind of inner peace that You were talking about when you said
"My peace I give to you" I want that.
Not the kind of peace that is the opposite of war,
But the kind of peace that is the opposite of fear.
The kind of peace that would allow me to let go of things,
Things like old grudges, my need to be right, needless worry, that
stuff.
Peace that would let me shut my head off at night and rest.

Then I asked Him what He wanted from me.
And please, I said, do not ask for total surrender.
I am not ready for some Suscipe type of giving.
No, He said, I will not ask for what you are not willing to give.
What I want from you is simply this:
I want you to be, just to be, the person my Father created you to be.
I sit for a minute and absorb this simplicity.
Is it really that simple? Why do I complicate things?
Gifts unwrapped, cookies unbaked, tree untrimmed.
No matter, I really am ready for Christmas this year.
Oh come, oh come Emmanuel, ransom captive me.

La Asombrosa
Lengua de Padre Bob

I lock my eyes on you, and follow your steps to the podium.
Knowing that the feast of words is about to begin,
I still myself and sit in quiet anticipation.
On this day in what way will I hear of the love of my God?
Will I hear of a love that existed before I was conceived?
A love so vast that it is far beyond my imagining.
Or will today be a story of infinite mercy and compassion?
What He has been willing to do - and still does - that I may
Share life in Him eternally.
Maybe this day there will be a new telling of an unimaginable
longing-
not of myself for God – of this I have already known - but more
incredibly
a telling of a longing I could never have imagined – that this
vast and mighty God could long for me.
My breath catches in my throat. This is too much!
Do you even know what your words do to me?
I want to devour and absorb them, to immerse myself in them
To savor and soak and steep in them.
Until your words become one with me and in me.
How I want so badly to hear them again and again and again.

You came to us last year with your enticing speech
Your alluring messages of love and hope and mercy
Do you see what you are doing to us?
You say that we are created out of His infinite love
And that He pursues a love relationship with us
You tell us that our lives are changed by God's sharing
His life with us
And of His longing for us just as we long for Him
You speak of the compassion our God has for us
Do you not see what you are doing to us?.
As our lives are changed we desire this for others.

As we feel the compassion of a loving God, we become healed
And desire healing compassion for each other.
As we become aware of His seductive love for us,
We desire this awareness of His love for each other.
Your words are opening not only our ears, but also our eyes.
As we hear of saints and prophets living ordinary lives,
We turn to see saints and prophets sitting in pews next to us.
Do you even see what you are doing to us?
Week after week, little by little, bit by bit,
You are transforming us into a holy people of God.

Breaking Open the Word

"Come with me and we shall break open the word."
He leads us down the long corridor, into the small meeting room.
Settling into my chair I wait, unsure what to expect.
Opening to John, and selecting the reading,
In his gentle voice he begins to read the passage.
I sit back and close my eyes, feel myself relax.
He begins softly, slowly
gentle words landing on my ears
And moving into my waiting mind.

I pray not only for them, but also for those who will believe in me
through their word, so that they may all be one, as you, Father, are
in me and I in You, that they also may be in us, that the world may
know that you sent me, And I have given them the glory you gave
me, so that they may be one as we are one, I in them and you in
me, that they may be brought to perfection as one, the world may
know that you sent me and that you love them even as you loved
me. Father, they are your gift to me

Just a minute
Am I hearing right?
Jesus is praying for us? We have been given His glory?
We may be one as they are one? I think he called us a gift.
We are gifts from the Father to Jesus?
Are you sure?
This just cannot be.
Read it again
This is too much!

I do not think, dear leader, that we have broken open the word
I think instead, that the word has broken open in us.

Abuela de Dios

Saint Ann do you know, I think of you often
Now that I am a grandmother too.
I wonder sometimes how it was for you
You waited and prayed so long for a child
Then you were finally rewarded with Mary.
After the angel visited
And you invited your husband into your body
Was something different about that time?
Did you know that he and you were creating
The Immaculate Conception?
Sometimes when I think of you, I see the window at
Immaculate Conception Church in Durham.
You and Joachim permanently etched in stained glass.

Were you a typical Jewish mom?
A little overprotective perhaps?
Mary wash your hands, Mary wear a coat, Mary eat your soup.
I bet she was such a good girl too.
You must have been shocked when
she told you she was pregnant.
Did you cry and tell her you were disappointed in her?
Did Joachim threaten to ground her for life?
And then Joseph threatened to divorce her
Before the wedding ceremony even took place.

When she was almost due to deliver,
They took off for Bethlehem.
They did not return home when expected
She did not call, she did not write, she did not email.
With no way to connect, you must have been worried sick.
Did you know all boy babies were being slaughtered?
I cannot imagine the sleepless nights, the endless worries.
And then one day they just showed up again in Nazareth,
Oh the joy you must have known.
You could put all worries and anxiety behind you, for they were
Bearing with them one perfect grandchild.
An incredible gift for you,
an incredible gift for all humankind.

All Knowing

Why? Why? Why?
Why me? Why my family? Why my job?
The wise man looked at me and replied with tenderness
"You are not the All Knowing."
"For some reason unknown to you, you are where you are meant
to be."
I took his words home with me and unwrapped them in my mind.
I do not know why my job, health, family are what they are.
But I find comfort in these words of wisdom,
"You are not the All Knowing."
There is a plan, and I did not make it.

I think of others whose history is a lesson to me,
Of Abraham, only able to see the now
Not able to envision the nation that would spring from his seed,
Yet acting with total trust
Never questioning the plan of the All Knowing,
He was willing to sacrifice his son in obedience.

I think of Mary, so confused she must have been by
Events of conception and childbirth.
and then the unimaginable pain,
Standing by as her innocent son was tried and tortured
She just kept saying yes, and going on in trust.
Accepting that she was not the All Knowing
She endured unspeakable pain.

Perhaps in a year or two or twenty
I will be able to see a purpose in this.
Where today all I see is pain and confusion.
But for now, I will take comfort in
The words of the wise man.
There is a plan and I did not make it.
I am where I am supposed to be.
I am not the All Knowing.

Be Mary for Me

Can you be Mary for me just for one day?
She does not solve, she does not advise
She simply listens
When the shepherds came to visit
on the morning of Christ's birth,
And said they had seen the star
Mary did not understand
But she listened and pondered
And kept these things in her heart

What did you hear me say to you?
All I wanted was to be heard and understood
Could you be Mary for me just for one day?
I did not seek unsolicited advice
I did not ask for you to fix me to your liking
When Jesus was presented in the temple
And Simeon blessed them and said to Mary
Your own soul a sword shall pierce,
Mary did not understand
But she held these words,
and pondered them in her heart

Please do not tell me what you have decided for me
What you think that I am asking of you
All I want is to be heard and understood
Would you be Mary for me just for one day?
When Jesus was lost in the temple,
Mary did not understand
Why he would say he had to be
about his Father's business
But she listened to him and took his words
And held them in her heart.
Could you please be Mary for me?
If only just for one day

On the Feast of the
Immaculate Conception

Oh Mary conceived without sin,
Today we celebrated this beautiful feast
Of your Immaculate Conception.
Remembering how God kept his promise to Ann and Joachim
By blessing their union with you.
While preparing you from your beginning,
To be a sinless human tabernacle.
The necessary preparation
For the Word to become flesh.

We read in the gospel of Luke
How the angel appeared to you
And told you that you had found favor with God.
Luke says you were greatly troubled
But the angel convinced you not to be afraid.
Mary, I am no angel, but I want to tell you
Follow your instincts, be very afraid
Mary, tell the angel, "No".

Please know that I want to protect you.
If you could just see what lies ahead.
If you tell the angel yes, you will have a son.
A beautiful child whom you will love
Beyond what you can imagine.
He will be perfect, unstained and holy.

And yet will cause a grief that will tear you apart.
Mary, you will live through pain that is unspeakable.
Your heart will break as you stand by helplessly and watch.
Your innocent son will be unjustly tried and convicted.
He will be spit upon, beaten without mercy,
Flogged until his skin hangs in bloody strips.
Mary, you cannot imagine the horror that will await you.

This perfect Son whom you will love, who is Love,
Will be stripped and placed on a wooden cross.
He will have huge nails driven through his hands and feet,
And he will be left to die a death of public humiliation.
Mary, you will stay with him, wishing you could trade places
with him
Like any mother would. But you cannot, you cannot do anything
But stand by helplessly in excruciating pain.

Mary, the choice is yours, save yourself and abandon us.
Mary, please just tell the angel, "No".

For Lent

What are you giving up for Lent? Adam asked of Eve.
Well, Eve said. I am thinking I should give up apples.
And what about you, husband of mine?
Adam replied, I think I am going to give up taking advice from you.
What are you giving up for Lent?
Abel asked his brother Cain?
Cain replied, I am going to try to give up my anger
Lest in a weak moment, I injure someone I love.
What are you giving up for Lent?
Jacob asked his twin, Esau.
Apparently my birthright, little brother of mine.
What are you giving up for Lent?
Moses asked of Aaron?
I am going to give up worshiping false gods
Especially the golden calf variety.
What about you? Aaron asked Moses in return.
I am giving up my need to see the promised land.
What are you giving up for lent?
Eliphaz, Bildad, and Zophar asked Job.
I am giving up trying to understand the mind of God.

What are you giving up for Lent? I asked of Mary.
She whispered her response so softly
I had to move in close to her to hear her hushed reply.

My only Son

Mary in the Mary Chapel

I saw Mary in the Mary chapel
she stood at the altar beside Father Bob
never speaking she told me of many things
she was awaiting the birth of her child she said
I looked at her in confusion
no crown of stars upon her head
no moon at her feet
no belly of pregnancy
hair untressed and in simple sandals shod
she stood expectantly like a waiting midwife
or a helpful labor coach
preparing for new life
no womanly giving of birth this time
no drop of sweat no pain no push
but a chosen man to bring new life
through his hands and voice
I saw with my own eyes
And I still do not understand
a birth by mystical mysterious words
this is My body
Mary gazed and smiled at Father Bob
and I knew it was completed now
that He had once again
allowed Himself to be among us
I saw Mary in the Mary chapel
beaming like a proud new mother
oh she said how she does love those

who bring to life again
her son on earth
it makes no sense to me and yet
I watched her as she smiled at me
come she said and meet my Son
take Him…..touch Him…..eat Him
and as I did she watched with pure delight
I still do not understand
but I wept with gratitude

Offertory

Just one drop of water
Yet a million believers
Poured into the wine
Tossing and tumbling
Swirling and Whirling
Merging and mingling
Dispersed and disseminated
Into this cup

By the mystery of this water
By the mystery of this wine
We ask for what we have been given
Our share in the divinity

Inebriated and intoxicated
Co-mingled and consecrated
Grace filled and grateful
Blessed and beatified

With mere words are we joined
Transformed and transubstantiated
Sacred and sacramental
We are the Body
We are the Blood
We are humanity we are divinity
The flesh made Word
In this mystical mystery

Transfused

Tonight at Mass I knelt under the big crucifix
Jesus suspended on overhead wire
He was in the usual on-the-cross pose
I looked at Him, His hands and feet and side
And remembered all of the times
That I had climbed in that wound in His side to rest
When life was cruel and I could not find comfort or consolation
Anywhere else.

I close my eyes
Once again I am enveloped in the warmth of His blood
Pressing slippery against me
Permeating my creases and pores
Penetrating me.
I am conscious of components
Plasma and platelets, red and white cells
wondering what blood type He has
(hoping He is type A like me).
Aware of blood adhering to my skin
I open my squinted eyes and look around
Like a newborn babe emerging from the bloody birthing hole
Fresh to the earth, newly from the womb.

I left the bloody hole of His side
I took my place in line
"Blood of Christ"
"Amen" then greedily I drank
Now I am saturated in His blood
Complete immersion inside and out
We stand for the final blessing
I am sent forth wholly, fully washed, renewed and cleansed.
The entire congregation responds with me, "Thanks be to God."

The Prodigal and Me

How many times have I heard this same parable?
The story of an elderly father and his 2 sons.
And always, always, always I am the prodigal.
Blowing dad's money, slopping pigs, crawling home
you know the story, you've heard it a hundred times too.
Today for the first time, this story has changed for me.
Today when I heard this story, my role was different,
I was the older brother who stayed home
slaving in the fields and tending the flocks.
When I complained about the prodigal and the party
I heard my father say these words to me
My son, you are with me always, and
Everything I have is yours………..
I must have heard wrong, please repeat
Everything I have is yours……..
Everything I have is yours………
Everything….. *Everything*…… *Everything*……..

Heavenly Father, I hear you say to me
Everything I have is yours.........
Your knowledge your wisdom
Are these mine Father?
Everything I have is yours.........
Even your glory Father, is that mine also?
What about your mercy and kindness,
Are those mine too?
Everything I have is yours.........
Your power and honor, your justice and truth
What about your faithfulness and goodness?
Everything I have is yours.........
Your divine nature, do I have it?
Am I made in your image and likeness?
Am I allowed a place in relationship with the Trinity?
Everything I have is yours.........

Heavenly Father, you tell me I am your beloved child
Give me the grace to receive these gifts with gratitude
Knowing I am heir of your divine essence
and that now, Father, I understand.
Everything You have is mine.........
Everything..... *Everything*...... *Everything*........

Snow Day

How many times have I promised
An hour of my life to You
And so set out to the Chapel of Adoration
With the best of intentions
Then while sitting in stillness before You
My head is filled
With those uninvited thoughts that
Pierce my resolve from every side
Replacing You with the mundane
Issues from daily life.

Well, today was payback
While trying to work from home.
The spreadsheet for review
- still waiting
Pushed aside by thoughts of You
The billing files to reconcile
-unexamined, unresolved
No match for You
You totally possessed me
Enticing me with beautiful speech
Seducing me with powerful promises

And who or what can compete?
There is no match for three of you
inviting me into relationship
Come you say and join us
How I do long for this union.
But I come with a lot of baggage.
Oh the usual history that you know yes,
But also I speak also for the others
To whom you have made this same promise
Beside myself, there are only
About seven billion or so
Of my closest brothers and sisters.

The Feast of Saint Stephen

I saw Jesus in the grocery store.
He was only born yesterday and yet there He was
One day old and all grown up
I read the New Testament but I do not remember
Reading that Jesus ever shopped in Harris Teeter.
While standing in the produce aisle
Hovering over a display of fruit
Deciding between oranges and tangerines
I saw Him approach
In a shy, hesitant manner.
In a very soft voice, He said simply "Ma'am".
I looked up from my citrus selecting
And orange in hand I responded, "Sir?"

Please He said, do not be afraid
I am homeless and have no place to sleep
(Just a minute, didn't we sing this yesterday?
"No crib for a bed". I do remember.)
I have not eaten, I am hungry.
He had in His hand His selected supper.
No pureed item from the infant aisle
But a box of crackers and a bottle of juice.
See, He said I have picked out items that are not expensive
Could you please buy my dinner tonight?
Sir, I replied, I would be honored.
How could I not embrace my chance to feed Him
When every day He feeds me with Himself.

The Gift

I peel and leave my self outside the door.
No place is this for usual world seen self.
Here true me enters naked and afraid.
I neatly fold and leave "her" on the shelf.

Acceptance is the ever present gift.
Relief is intermingled with cold fright.
Truth so deeply longed for hungrily sought.
Lacks consolation in exposed harsh light

Here tears flow as the buried is unearthed.
And memory exhumed is pain exposed.
Here inmost self is cracked to cries of rage.
No longer head nor heart permitted closed.

The language of your body conveys safe.
Your spoken words are chosen with such care.
They float to me and secret in my mind.
Conversing with my thoughts then resting there.

Diverting from the goals that first I sought.
To such I did not know I could explore.
I stood outside and begged of you to guide.
You took my hand and led me to my core.

Who is this new found woman introduced?
A long familiar recall floats in mist.
The jolt of realization it's herself.
Created one that God could not resist.

The Kingdom of God

Even as children we were told we had a role in
In building the Kingdom of God.
Do this, don't do that
You need to remember that
You are building the Kingdom of God.
Such a heavy role, such a burden
Weighing each decision as though the
Kingdom of God depended on me.
So fearful of mistakes
In fulfilling my Kingdom obligations.

But as for Your Kingdom now, Lord,
Pardon me for being so outspoken
But the truth is this,
For years I have worried about my role in
Bringing about Your kingdom
And I am just plain exhausted.
So if I may be blunt with you,
I would like to say
It's Your damn Kingdom
Build it Yourself.

Things I Like About You, God

Lord do you know
I have been thinking
About how much we have in common

I am fully human
So were you
I like that in a God.

I have been totally beaten and broken
So have you
I like that in a God.

All humans die, so will I
You went first
I like that in a God.

You have a nice mom
You share her with me
I like that in a God.

You are totally divine
You impart that to me
I like that in a God

You are eternal life
You give that to me
I like that in a God.

Eavesdropping

Lord, I did not mean to eavesdrop
But now I'm glad I did
I heard you talking to your Father
Thanking Him for the gift
So special and unique
like none other you have known
And how you love and treasure this
beyond human comprehension

And then you saw me there
And knew I had overheard
So when you turned to me
I knew then that you realized
That I already knew
The gift of which you spoke
Created by your Father
Is me

Made in the USA
Lexington, KY
02 June 2013